GET THE ANSWERS! History

Q&A ABOUT THE FRENCH AND INDIAN WAR

By Benjamin Proudfit

INVESTIGATE!

Enslow PUBLISHING

Please visit our website, www.enslow.com. For a free color catalog of all our high-quality books, call toll free 1-800-398-2504 or fax 1-877-980-4454.

Library of Congress Cataloging-in-Publication Data

Names: Proudfit, Benjamin, author.
Title: Q & A about the French and Indian War / Benjamin Proudfit.
Other titles: Questions and answers about the French and Indian War
Description: Buffalo, New York : Enslow Publishing, [2026] | Series: Get the answers! : History | Includes bibliographical references and index. | Audience: Grades 2-3
Identifiers: LCCN 2024054593 (print) | LCCN 2024054594 (ebook) | ISBN 9781978544345 (library binding) | ISBN 9781978544338 (paperback) | ISBN 9781978544352 (ebook)
Subjects: LCSH: United States–History–French and Indian War, 1754-1763–Miscellanea–Juvenile literature.
Classification: LCC E199 .P948 2026 (print) | LCC E199 (ebook) | DDC 973.2/6–dc23/eng/20250124
LC record available at https://lccn.loc.gov/2024054593
LC ebook record available at https://lccn.loc.gov/2024054594

Published in 2026 by
Enslow Publishing
2544 Clinton Street
Buffalo, NY 14224

Designer: Andrea Davison-Bartolotta
Editor: Kristen Nelson

Photo credits: Cover, pp. 1, 10 , 14, 22, 24, 25 (bottom) courtesy of Library of Congress; series art (question mark backgrounds) Darcraft/Shutterstock.com; p. 5 (background) SveKo/Shutterstock.com; p. 5 (map) File:Nouvelle-France map-en.svg/Wikimedia Commons; p. 6 File:Iroquois western goods.jpg/Wikimedia Commons; p. 7 File:Vue du debarquement anglais pour lattaque de Louisbourg 1745.jpg/Wikimedia Commons; pp. 8, 19 Peter Hermes Furian/Shutterstock.com; p. 9 Museums at Washington and Lee University; p. 11 Bibliotheque et Archives Nationales Du Quebec; p. 12 EWY Media/Shutterstock.com; p. 13 File:Alexander von Kotzebue - Battle of Kunersdorf on 1 August 1759.jpg/Wikimedia Commons; p. 15 © GrandPalaisRmn (Château de Versailles); p. 16 tokar/Shutterstock.com; pp. 17, 23 courtesy of The Metropolitan Museum of Art; p. 18 National Portrait Gallery, Smithsonian Institution; p. 20 File:New Map of North America (1763).JPG/Wikimedia Commons; p. 25 (top) Everett Collection/Shutterstock.com; p. 26 North Wind Picture Archives/Alamy Stock Photo; p. 27 File:Map of territorial growth 1775.svg/Wikimedia Commons; p. 29 powerofforever/iStockphoto.com.

Printed in the United States of America

CPSIA compliance information: Batch #CS26ENS: For further information contact Enslow Publishing, at 1-800-398-2504.

CONTENTS

Words in the glossary appear in **bold** type the first time they are used in the text.

SETTLING NORTH AMERICA

The first European settlements in North America were established in present-day Florida in the 1560s. Both France and Spain claimed land there, though Spain soon pushed France out. The first permanent, or lasting, British colony was Jamestown, founded in 1607. France established Quebec in present-day Canada the following year.

By the 1750s, both Great Britain and France had greatly **expanded** their holdings in North America. However, they also both wanted to grow more. This led to war!

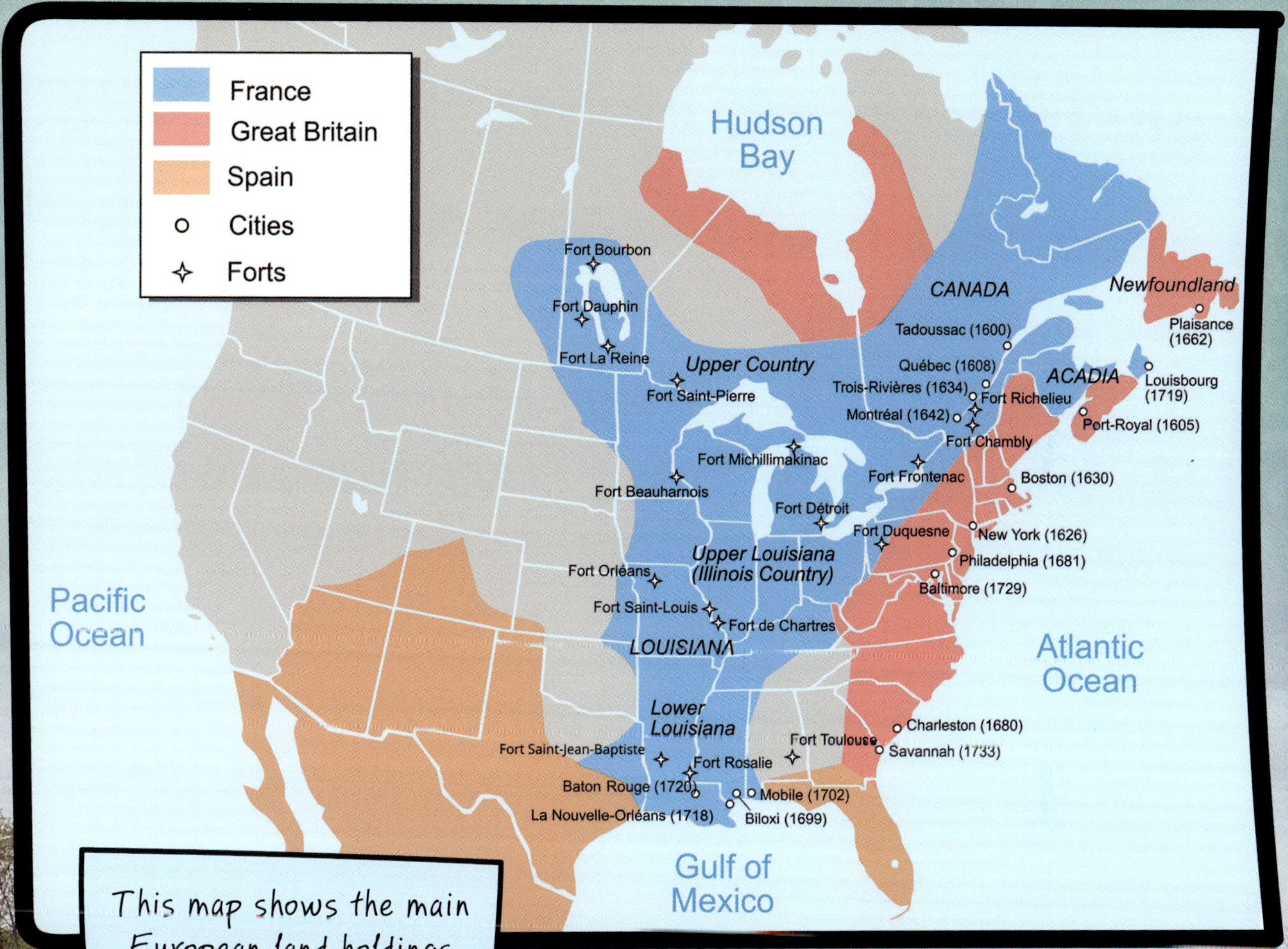

This map shows the main European land holdings around 1755.

THE STARTING POINTS

QUESTION 1

Who settled North American land first?

ANSWER

It wasn't Europeans! Native Americans had been living in North America for thousands of years. In fact, European settlers often pushed Native groups off their land. However, some Native groups did work with European settlers, including in trade and war.

Iroquois with colonial goods they traded for

QUESTION 2

Did France and Great Britain get along?

ANSWER

These countries had been at war on and off for years. The fighting that took place in North America included King William's War (1689–1697), Queen Anne's War (1702–1712), and King George's War (1744–1748).

Earlier **conflicts** between France and Great Britain also had to do with who would have control over parts of North America.

QUESTION 3

What happened in the Ohio River Valley?

ANSWER

Both colonists in New France and the British colony of Virginia believed the land of the Ohio River Valley belonged to them. Then, France began building forts in the area. They wanted a better claim to the land. The British were not happy.

The French population had grown a lot in the early 1700s. That's partly why they moved closer to the Ohio River, shown here in the present-day United States.

QUESTION 4

How did George Washington play a part?

ANSWER

In 1753, Washington said he would take a message to the French for Virginia's governor. The message told the French to stop building Fort LeBoeuf in Pennsylvania and to leave the Ohio River Valley. If the French didn't, they would be attacked.

Washington was a 21-year-old in the Virginia **Militia** at the time the French and Indian War began.

WAR BEGINS

QUESTION 5

What started the war?

ANSWER

The French wouldn't leave the Ohio River Valley. Virginia's governor ordered British forts to be built. He **promoted** Washington and sent him to force the French out. Both the French and British began working to gather **allies** in nearby Native American groups.

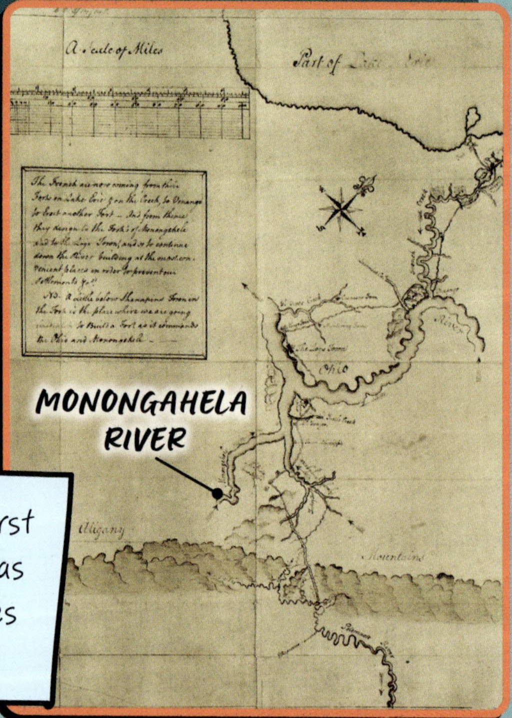

The Battle of Jumonville Glen was the first battle of the French and Indian War. It was fought on May 28, 1754, about 20 miles (32 km) from the Monongahela River.

QUESTION 6

Which Native American groups sided with which European power?

ANSWER

The **Iroquois Confederacy** sided with the British. The Delaware, Ottawa, and Shawnee, among others, sided with the French. Native allies came to be more important to the French who had fewer troops than the British.

Native American groups fought each other as allies of the British and French in the French and Indian War.

QUESTION 7

What was Fort Necessity?

ANSWER

This poorly built "fort" was used by Washington and his forces in the Ohio River Valley shortly after the Battle of Jumonville Glen. In the Battle of Fort Necessity on July 3, 1754, both sides lost many men. However, Washington and his troops ultimately lost.

This present-day reconstruction of Fort Necessity shows how weak this "fort" likely was.

EUROPE TAKES PART

QUESTION 8

What was the Seven Years' War?

ANSWER

The fighting in North America was part of conflicts between Great Britain and France and their allies around the world. They fought for control of colonies in India too. Russia, Austria, and Sweden took part on France's side. Prussia and Hanover were British allies.

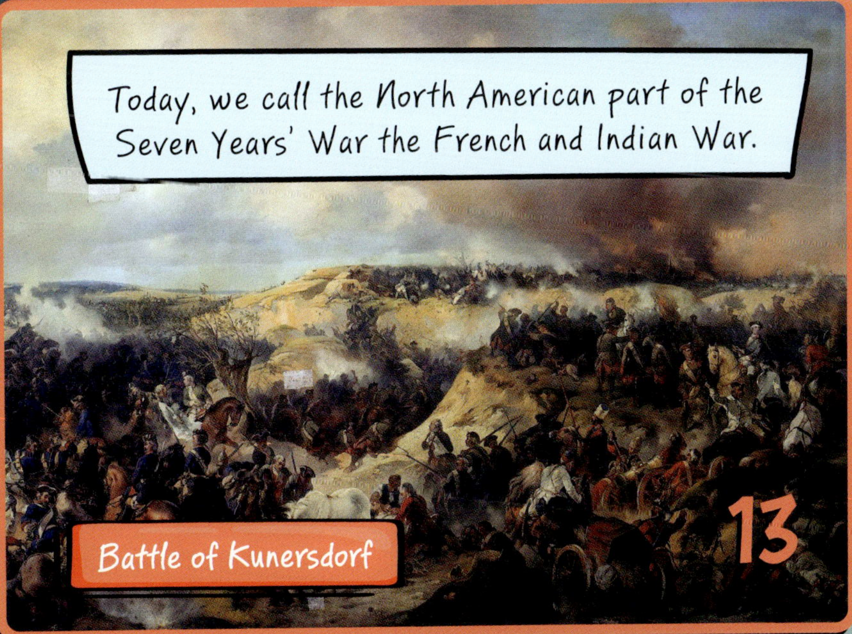

Today, we call the North American part of the Seven Years' War the French and Indian War.

Battle of Kunersdorf

QUESTION 9

Why was General Edward Braddock sent to the colonies?

ANSWER

Washington's efforts to stop the French had failed. The British government sent Braddock to lead the British forces and allies in North America. Colonial leaders wouldn't follow him, however. The British lost important battles under his command.

Edward Braddock died in 1755 during a battle near Pittsburgh, Pennsylvania. He is commonly blamed for the British being unable to push the French out of the Ohio River Valley early in the war.

What is a stalemate?

ANSWER

It is a time during a conflict when neither side can make good progress. This happened between the French and British in North America shortly after the war started. However, fighting between them continued in other places around the world.

The French bested Great Britain in the Mediterranean in 1756.

INTO CANADA

QUESTION 11

What turned the tide of the war?

ANSWER

In 1758, the British began attacking French forts in Canada. They took Fort Niagara and Fort Carillon the next year. Finally, the British defeated the French in Quebec. This was the final blow to the French in North America.

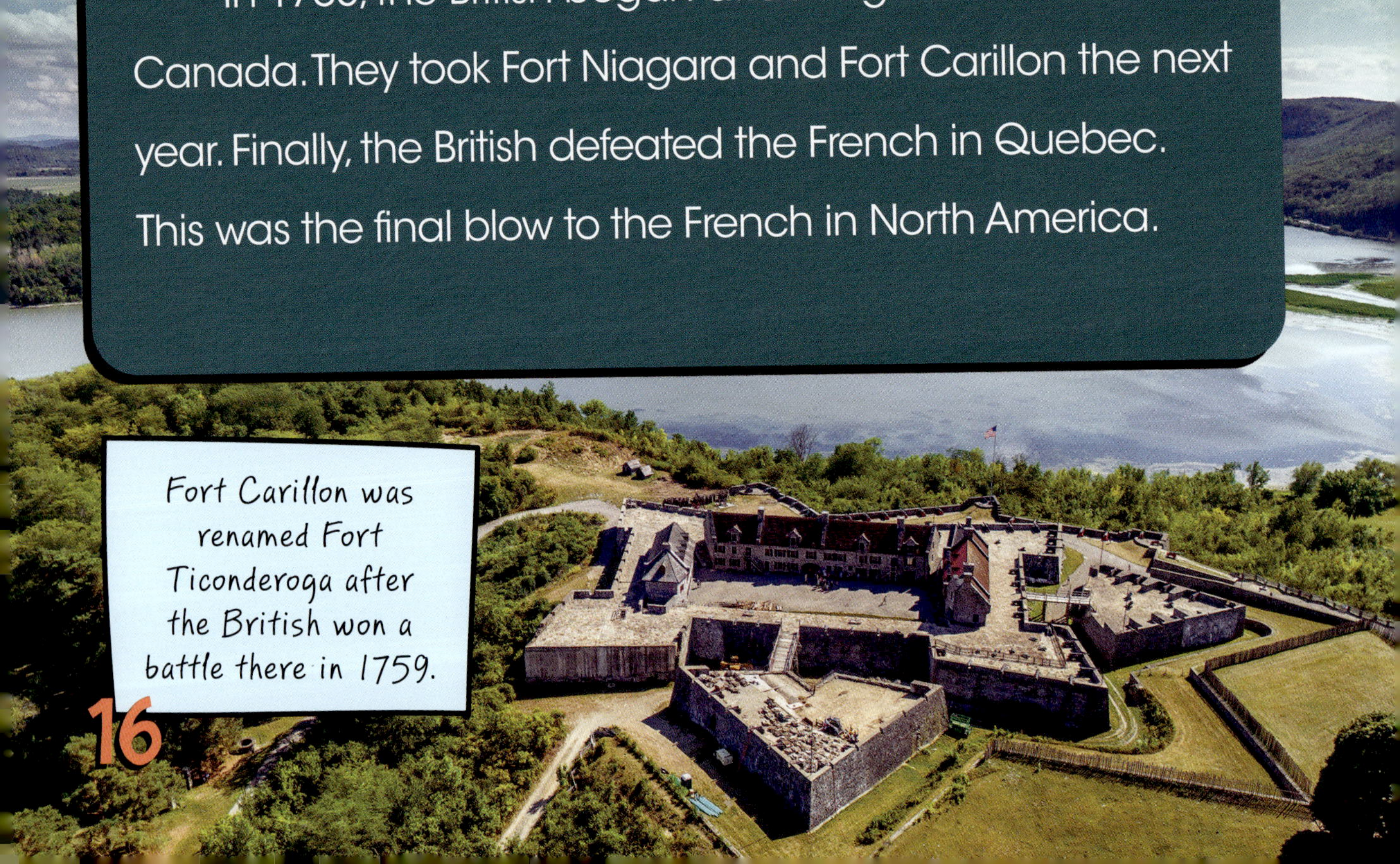

Fort Carillon was renamed Fort Ticonderoga after the British won a battle there in 1759.

QUESTION 12

Why didn't the first peace talks work?

ANSWER

France tried to start peace talks after the British took Canada. But Great Britain asked for more than the French government was willing to give, including the whole of Canada. The **negotiations** failed.

Louis XV, king of France from 1715 to 1744

SPAIN STEPS IN

QUESTION 13

Why did Spain get involved?

ANSWER

Spain's king, Charles III, was cousin of France's king, Louis XV. The two countries signed the Family Compact in August 1761. It said that Spain would declare war on Great Britain in May 1762 if the war wasn't over yet.

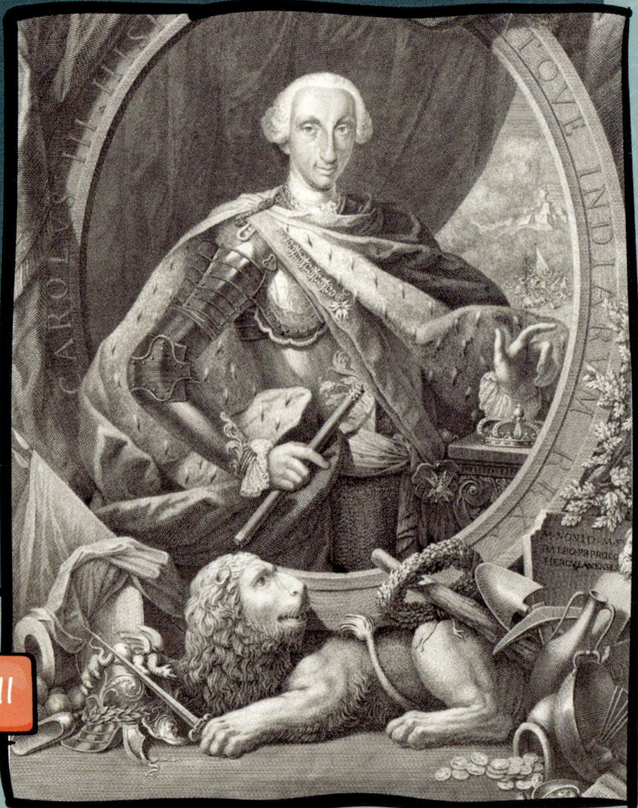

King Charles III

QUESTION 14

Did Spain truly help France?

ANSWER

The Family Compact was supposed to push Great Britain into peace talks. It didn't. Instead, Great Britain declared war on Spain. The British then took Cuba, which was Spanish territory, in August 1762.

The British Navy was very strong. It took not only Cuba from Spain, but also Caribbean islands and the Philippines from France.

A TREATY IS SIGNED

QUESTION 15

What ended the war?

ANSWER

Great Britain signed the **Treaty** of Paris with France and its allies on February 10, 1763. The treaty shifted the power in North America almost entirely to Great Britain.

The Treaty of Paris

- France took back control of the islands of Martinque, St. Lucia, and Guadeloupe in the Caribbean.
- France lost all its North American claims east of the Mississippi River to Great Britain.
- France lost Canada to Great Britain.
- Spain lost Florida to Great Britain.
- Spain took back control of Cuba.
- Spain gained French territory west of the Mississippi, including the port of New Orleans.

The Treaty of Paris ended the Seven Years' War, including the North American part now called the French and Indian War.

EFFECTS ON WASHINGTON

QUESTION 16

How did the French and Indian War shape George Washington's reputation?

ANSWER

Washington had little military **experience** when the war began. He went on to command the Virginia Militia for a time. This made him a well-known and well-respected figure in the colonies.

QUESTION 17

Did the war shape Washington's ideas about Great Britain?

ANSWER

Yes. Washington resigned, or left, the Virginia Militia in 1758. It was partly due to his inability to get an equal position in the British Army. Following the war, he began to disagree more with how the British treated the colonies.

Washington's experience in the French and Indian War led to his position as commander of the colonial army during the American Revolution.

EFFECTS ON THE COLONIES

QUESTION 18

How did the end of the war affect the colonies?

ANSWER

Great Britain was in great **debt** following the French and Indian War. It began taxing the colonies to make up some of that money. This made many colonists angry.

tarring and feathering a tax collector

Taxing the Colonies

1764 Sugar Act
raised taxes on goods shipped to the colonies that weren't from Great Britain

1765 Stamp Act
taxed mostly paper goods such as newspapers and playing cards. It was repealed, or canceled, in 1766.

1767 Townshend Acts
taxed glass, lead, paint, paper, and tea

tax stamps

fighting the Stamp Act

QUESTION 19

What was the state of the relationship between Great Britain, the colonies, and Native groups after the war?

ANSWER

The British began forcing Native groups to give up land. Colonists continued to move onto Native American land too. This led to war with Native groups between 1763 and 1764 as well as fighting with the colonies for years after.

QUESTION 20

What was the Proclamation of 1763?

ANSWER

The British government tried to stop colonists from settling on Native American land past the Appalachian Mountains. Colonists who lived there already were told to leave. It also set up a Native American reservation, or area of land just for Native groups.

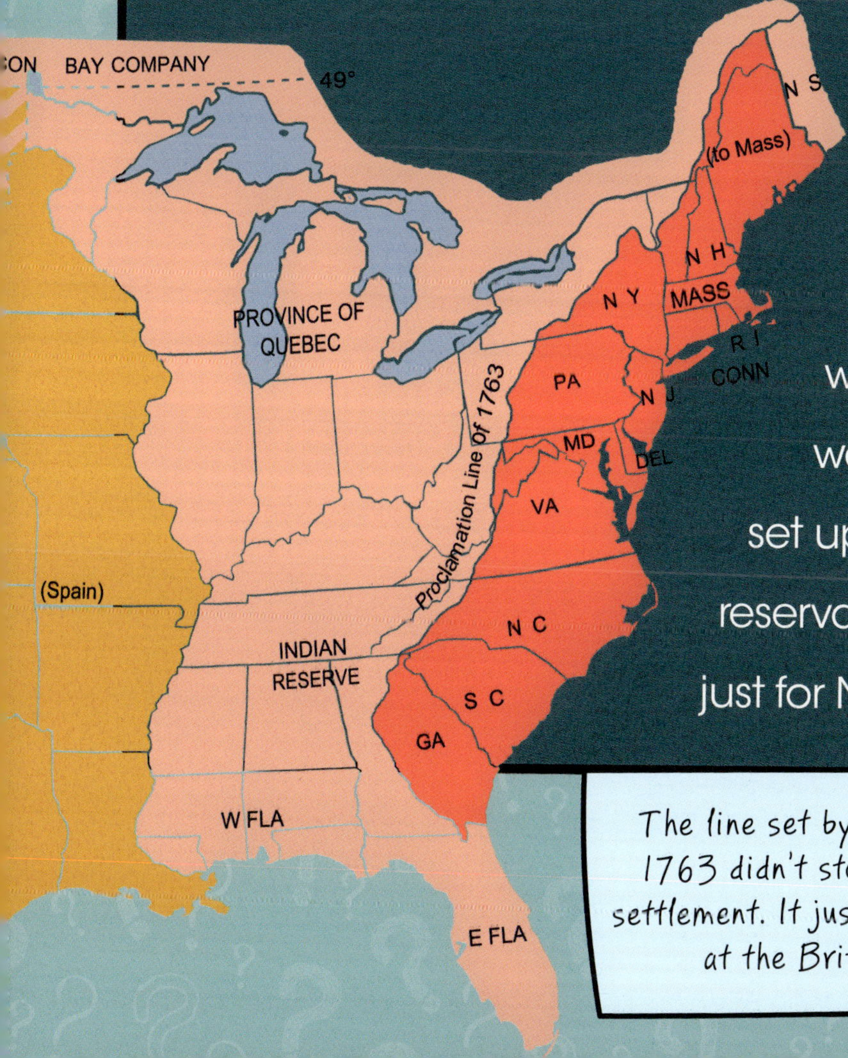

The line set by the Proclamation of 1763 didn't stop colonist's western settlement. It just made them more mad at the British government!

ONE WAR LEADS TO ANOTHER

The end of the French and Indian War changed the makeup of North America. British ideas and ways of life became the greatest European **influence** on the colonies there. English became the main language spoken too.

However, the taxes passed after the war, as well as other laws, angered colonists into the 1770s. These became one of the main causes of the American Revolution, the war in which the 13 British colonies won their freedom from Great Britain.

The American Revolution was fought from 1775 to 1783.

GLOSSARY

ally: One of two or more people or groups who work together.

conflict: A fight.

debt: An amount of money owed.

expand: To get larger and looser.

experience: Having skills gained by doing something.

influence: To have an effect on.

Iroquois Confederacy: A group of Native American tribes living in present-day New York who worked and acted together.

militia: A group of citizens who organize like soldiers in order to protect themselves.

negotiate: To come to an agreement.

promote: To raise someone in rank.

relationship: A connection to another person or group.

reputation: The views that are held about something or someone.

treaty: An agreement between countries.

FOR MORE INFORMATION

BOOKS

Hansen, Grace. *Living in Colonial America*. Minneapolis, MN: Pop!, 2024.

Knopp, Erza E. *Myths and Facts About George Washington*. Buffalo, NY: PowerKids Press, 2024.

Walton, Kathryn. *The French and Indian War*. Buffalo, NY: Enslow Publishing, 2024.

WEBSITES

Colonial America
https://www.ducksters.com/history/colonial_america/
Find out about how the North American colonies were founded.

French and Indian War
https://kids.britannica.com/kids/article/French-and-Indian-War/353151
Read more about the French and Indian War here.

Teach Dear America
https://www.scholastic.com/teachdearamerica/colonial.htm
Follow the timeline to learn more about U.S. history around the time of the French and Indian War.

INDEX